Recipes to make your own giving

Use these recipes to delight your friends and family. Each recipe includes gift tags for your convenience – just cut them out and personalize. After personalizing your tag, attach it to the bottle using raffia, ribbon, twine or yarn.

Use a variety of different bottle sizes and shapes according to your tastes. Depending on the size of the recipe and bottles you use, you may be able to fill 1, 2 or even 3 bottles. Decorative bottles can be found at craft or import stores. (Or keep your eyes open at garage sales and flea markets!)

Printed in the United States of America
by G&R Publishing Co.

Distributed By:

507 Industrial Street
Waverly, IA 50677

ISBN 1-56383-172-4
Item # 3430

Blackberry Vinegar

Makes 1 quart

1 C. blackberries
3 C. apple cider vinegar
2 T. sugar

Wash blackberries thoroughly under running water and pat dry. In a medium bowl, combine vinegar, cleaned blackberries and sugar. Mix gently until sugar dissolves. Using a funnel, transfer to a decorative sealable bottle. Cover bottle tightly and store in refrigerator.

Attach a gift tag with directions on how to serve vinegar.

Gift Tag Directions:

Blackberry Vinegar

Toss Blackberry Vinegar with salad greens or use as a dipping sauce for bread. Store in refrigerator.

Blackberry Vinegar

Toss Blackberry Vinegar with salad greens or use as a dipping sauce for bread. Store in refrigerator.

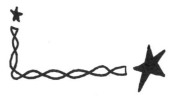

Blackberry Vinegar

Toss Blackberry Vinegar with salad greens or use as a dipping sauce for bread. Store in refrigerator.

Blackberry Vinegar

Toss Blackberry Vinegar with salad greens or use as a dipping sauce for bread. Store in refrigerator.

Blackberry Vinegar

Toss Blackberry Vinegar with salad greens or use as a dipping sauce for bread. Store in refrigerator.

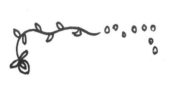

Rosemary Thyme Vinegar

Makes 1 quart

2 sprigs fresh rosemary
2 sprigs fresh thyme
4 C. distilled white vinegar
1/3 C. water

Wash rosemary and thyme sprigs thoroughly under running water and pat dry. Place clean rosemary and thyme sprigs in a decorative sealable bottle. In a large saucepan over medium heat, bring vinegar and water almost to boiling point and remove from heat. Using a funnel, transfer vinegar to bottle with rosemary and thyme. Cover bottle tightly and store in refrigerator.

Attach a gift tag with directions on how to serve vinegar.

Gift Tag Directions:

Rosemary Thyme Vinegar

Toss Rosemary Thyme Vinegar with salad greens or use as a dipping sauce for bread. Store in refrigerator.

Rosemary Thyme Vinegar

Toss Rosemary Thyme Vinegar with salad greens or use as a dipping sauce for bread. Store in refrigerator.

Rosemary Thyme Vinegar

Toss Rosemary Thyme Vinegar with salad greens or use as a dipping sauce for bread. Store in refrigerator.

**Rosemary Thyme
Vinegar**

Toss Rosemary
Thyme Vinegar with
salad greens or use
as a dipping sauce
for bread. Store in
refrigerator.

**Rosemary Thyme
Vinegar**

Toss Rosemary
Thyme Vinegar with
salad greens or use
as a dipping sauce
for bread. Store in
refrigerator.

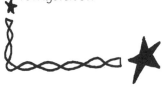

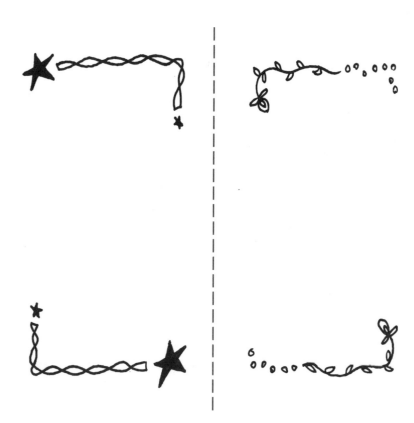

Fresh Dill Vinegar

Makes 1 quart

2 to 3 sprigs fresh dill
Peel of 1 lemon (peeled in a spiral)
1/2 tsp. whole black peppercorns
4 C. distilled white vinegar

Wash dill sprigs thoroughly under running water and pat dry. Place clean dill sprigs, lemon peel and whole black peppercorns in a decorative sealable bottle. In a large saucepan over medium heat, bring vinegar almost to boiling point. Remove from heat. Using a funnel, transfer vinegar to bottle with dill, lemon peel and peppercorns. Cover bottle tightly and store in refrigerator.

Attach a gift tag with directions on how to serve vinegar.

Gift Tag Directions:

Fresh Dill Vinegar

Toss Fresh Dill Vinegar
with salad greens or use as a
marinade for fresh seafood.
Store in refrigerator.

Fresh Dill Vinegar

Toss Fresh Dill Vinegar with salad greens or use as a marinade for fresh seafood. Store in refrigerator.

Fresh Dill Vinegar

Toss Fresh Dill Vinegar with salad greens or use as a marinade for fresh seafood. Store in refrigerator.

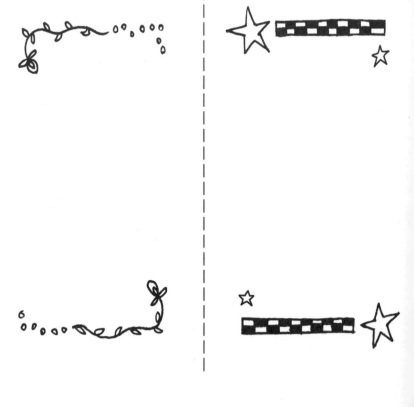

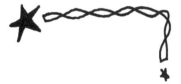

Fresh Dill Vinegar

Toss Fresh Dill
Vinegar with salad
greens or use as a
marinade for fresh
seafood. Store in
refrigerator.

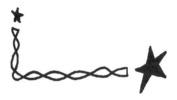

Fresh Dill Vinegar

Toss Fresh Dill
Vinegar with salad
greens or use as a
marinade for fresh
seafood. Store in
refrigerator.

Herbal Vinegar

Makes 1 quart

3 to 4 sprigs fresh parsley
2 tsp. dried thyme leaves
1 tsp. dried rosemary leaves
1 tsp. dried sage leaves
4 C. red wine vinegar

Wash fresh parsley thoroughly under running water and pat dry. Place clean parsley sprigs, dried thyme, dried rosemary and dried sage in a decorative sealable bottle. In a large saucepan over medium heat, bring vinegar almost to boiling point. Remove from heat. Using a funnel, transfer vinegar to bottle with parsley sprigs and dried herbs. Cover bottle tightly and store in refrigerator.

Attach a gift tag with directions on how to serve vinegar.

Gift Tag Directions:

Herbal Vinegar

Toss Herbal Vinegar with salad greens or use as a marinade for fresh seafood. Store in refrigerator.

Herbal Vinegar

Toss Herbal Vinegar with salad greens or use as a marinade for fresh seafood. Store in refrigerator.

Herbal Vinegar

Toss Herbal Vinegar with salad greens or use as a marinade for fresh seafood. Store in refrigerator.

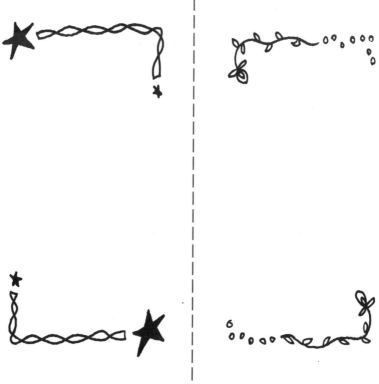

Herbal Vinegar

Toss Herbal Vinegar with salad greens or use as a marinade for fresh seafood. Store in refrigerator.

Herbal Vinegar

Toss Herbal Vinegar with salad greens or use as a marinade for fresh seafood. Store in refrigerator.

Raspberry Vinegar

Makes 1 quart

2 C. raspberries
2 C. distilled white or white wine vinegar

Wash raspberries under running water and pat dry. Bruise raspberries slightly and place in a decorative sealable bottle. In a large saucepan over medium heat, bring vinegar almost to boiling point. Remove from heat. Using a funnel, transfer vinegar to bottle with raspberries. Cover bottle tightly and store in refrigerator.

Attach a gift tag with directions on how to serve vinegar.

Gift Tag Directions:

Raspberry Vinegar

Toss Raspberry Vinegar with salad greens or fresh fruits. Store in refrigerator.

Raspberry Vinegar

Toss Raspberry Vinegar with salad greens or fresh fruits. Store in refrigerator.

Raspberry Vinegar

Toss Raspberry Vinegar with salad greens or fresh fruits. Store in refrigerator.

Raspberry Vinegar

Toss Raspberry
Vinegar with salad
greens or fresh
fruits. Store in
refrigerator.

Raspberry Vinegar

Toss Raspberry
Vinegar with salad
greens or fresh
fruits. Store in
refrigerator.

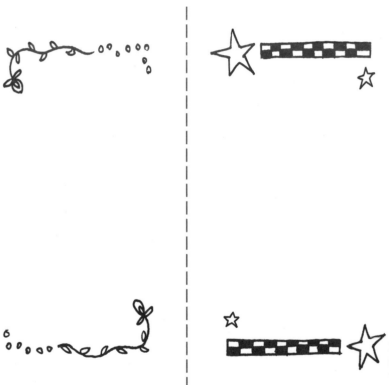

Cranberry Vinegar

Makes 3 cups

4 C. white wine or apple cider vinegar
1 1/2 C. fresh or frozen and thawed
    cranberries, divided
6 T. honey
1 cinnamon stick
2 whole cloves

In a medium saucepan over medium heat, bring vinegar and half of the cranberries to a boil. Reduce heat and let simmer for 2 minutes. Add honey and mix well. Strain cranberry mixture through a strainer, pressing out as much liquid as possible. Using a funnel, transfer vinegar to a decorative sealable bottle. Add remaining half of cranberries, cinnamon stick and cloves to bottle. Cover bottle tightly and store in refrigerator.

Attach a gift tag with directions on how to serve vinegar.

Gift Tag Directions:

Cranberry Vinegar

Toss Cranberry Vinegar with salad greens or use as a marinade for chicken or turkey. Store in refrigerator.

Cranberry Vinegar

Toss Cranberry Vinegar with salad greens or use as a marinade for chicken or turkey. Store in refrigerator.

Cranberry Vinegar

Toss Cranberry Vinegar with salad greens or use as a marinade for chicken or turkey. Store in refrigerator.

Cranberry Vinegar

Toss Cranberry Vinegar with salad greens or use as a marinade for chicken or turkey. Store in refrigerator.

Cranberry Vinegar

Toss Cranberry Vinegar with salad greens or use as a marinade for chicken or turkey. Store in refrigerator.

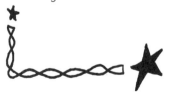

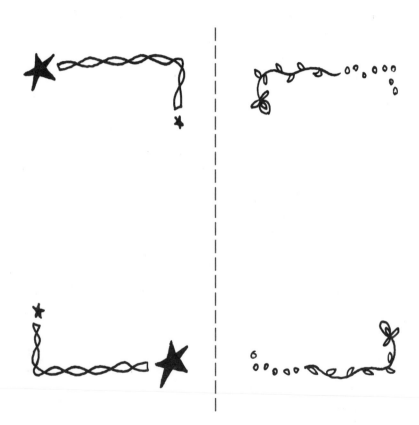

Lemon Mint Vinegar

Makes 2 cups

1 lemon
1/4 C. chopped fresh mint leaves
2 C. white wine vinegar

Cut peel from lemon in a continuous spiral and place peel in a jar with a lid. Add chopped mint leaves to jar. In a medium saucepan over medium heat, bring vinegar to a boil. Pour vinegar over lemon peel and mint leaves in jar. Cover and let stand for 2 weeks. Using a funnel, transfer vinegar to a decorative sealable bottle, removing lemon peel and mint leaves. Add fresh lemon peel and fresh mint leaves to bottle. Cover bottle tightly and store in refrigerator.

Attach a gift tag with directions on how to serve vinegar.

Gift Tag Directions:

Lemon Mint Vinegar

Toss Lemon Mint Vinegar with salad greens or pour over steamed vegetables or fresh fruit salad. Store in refrigerator.

Lemon Mint Vinegar

Toss Lemon Mint
Vinegar with salad
greens or pour over
steamed vegetables
or fresh fruit salad.
Store in refrigerator.

Lemon Mint Vinegar

Toss Lemon Mint
Vinegar with salad
greens or pour over
steamed vegetables
or fresh fruit salad.
Store in refrigerator.

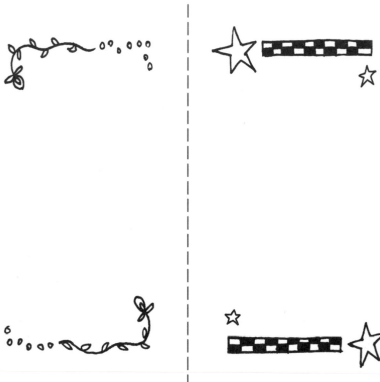

Lemon Mint Vinegar

Toss Lemon Mint
Vinegar with salad
greens or pour over
steamed vegetables
or fresh fruit salad.
Store in refrigerator.

Lemon Mint Vinegar

Toss Lemon Mint
Vinegar with salad
greens or pour over
steamed vegetables
or fresh fruit salad.
Store in refrigerator.

Creamy Italian Dressing

Makes 1 1/2 cups

1 C. mayonnaise
1/4 C. chopped onions
2 T. red wine vinegar
1 T. sugar
3/4 tsp. Italian seasoning
1/4 tsp. garlic powder
1/4 tsp. salt
1/8 tsp. pepper

In a blender or food processor, combine mayonnaise, onions, vinegar and sugar. Add Italian seasoning, garlic powder, salt and pepper. Blend until smooth. Using a funnel, transfer to a decorative sealable bottle and refrigerate. Will keep for 5 to 7 days in the refrigerator.

Attach a gift tag with directions on how to serve dressing.

Gift Tag Directions:

Creamy Italian Dressing

Toss Creamy Italian Dressing with salad greens or use as a dipping sauce for bread. Store in refrigerator and discard after 5 to 7 days.

Creamy Italian Dressing

Toss Creamy Italian Dressing with salad greens or use as a dipping sauce for bread. Store in refrigerator and discard after 5 to 7 days.

Creamy Italian Dressing

Toss Creamy Italian Dressing with salad greens or use as a dipping sauce for bread. Store in refrigerator and discard after 5 to 7 days.

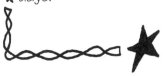

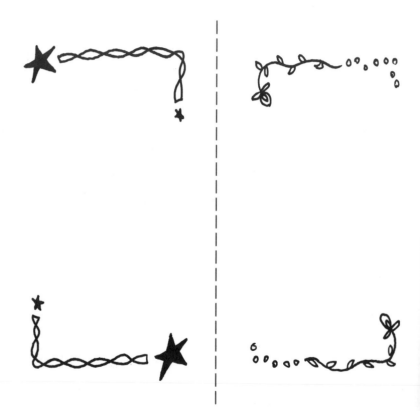

Creamy Italian Dressing

Toss Creamy Italian Dressing with salad greens or use as a dipping sauce for bread. Store in refrigerator and discard after 5 to 7 days.

Creamy Italian Dressing

Toss Creamy Italian Dressing with salad greens or use as a dipping sauce for bread. Store in refrigerator and discard after 5 to 7 days.

Ranch Dressing

Makes 1 1/2 cups

1 C. mayonnaise
1/2 C. sour cream
1/2 tsp. dried chives
1/2 tsp. dried parsley flakes
1/2 tsp. dried dillweed
1/4 tsp. ground garlic
1/4 tsp. onion powder
1/8 tsp. salt
1/8 tsp. pepper

In a large bowl, whisk together mayonnaise, sour cream, dried chives, dried parsley flakes, dried dillweed, ground garlic, onion powder, salt and pepper. Using a funnel, transfer to a decorative sealable bottle and refrigerate. Will keep for 7 to 10 days in the refrigerator.

Attach a gift tag with directions on how to serve dressing.

Gift Tag Directions:

Ranch Dressing

Toss Ranch Dressing with salad greens or use as a dipping sauce for veggies. Store in refrigerator and discard after 7 to 10 days.

Ranch Dressing

Toss Ranch
Dressing with
salad greens or use
as a dipping sauce
for veggies. Store
in refrigerator and
discard after 7 to
10 days.

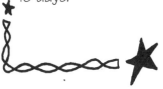

Ranch Dressing

Toss Ranch
Dressing with
salad greens or use
as a dipping sauce
for veggies. Store
in refrigerator and
discard after 7 to
10 days.

Ranch Dressing

Toss Ranch
Dressing with
salad greens or use
as a dipping sauce
for veggies. Store
in refrigerator and
discard after 7 to
10 days.

Ranch Dressing

Toss Ranch
Dressing with
salad greens or use
as a dipping sauce
for veggies. Store
in refrigerator and
discard after 7 to
10 days.

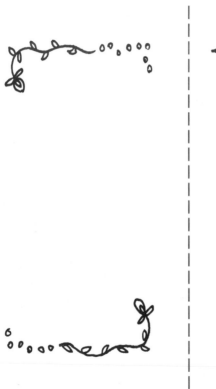

Thousand Island Dressing

Makes 1 1/2 cups

2/3 C. mayonnaise
2/3 C. plain yogurt
1 T. apple cider vinegar
Pinch of paprika
2 T. ketchup
10 pimento-stuffed olives,
    finely chopped

1 tsp. dried chopped chives
1/2 tsp. dried parsley flakes
1 clove garlic, minced
Salt and pepper
Milk, optional

In a large bowl, combine mayonnaise, plain yogurt, vinegar, paprika, ketchup, finely chopped olives, dried chopped chives, parsley flakes and minced garlic. Mix until well blended. Add salt and pepper to taste. If a thinner sauce is desired, add a little milk. Using a funnel, transfer to a decorative sealable bottle and refrigerate. Will keep for 5 to 7 days in the refrigerator.

Attach a gift tag with directions on how to serve dressing.

Gift Tag Directions:

Thousand Island Dressing

Toss Thousand Island Dressing with salad greens or use as a dipping sauce for vegetables. Store in refrigerator and discard after 5 to 7 days.

Thousand Island Dressing

Toss Thousand Island Dressing with salad greens or use as a dipping sauce for vegetables. Store in refrigerator and discard after 5 to 7 days.

Thousand Island Dressing

Toss Thousand Island Dressing with salad greens or use as a dipping sauce for vegetables. Store in refrigerator and discard after 5 to 7 days.

**Thousand Island
Dressing**

Toss Thousand
Island Dressing with
salad greens or use
as a dipping sauce
for vegetables. Store
in refrigerator and
discard after 5 to 7
days.

**Thousand Island
Dressing**

Toss Thousand
Island Dressing with
salad greens or use
as a dipping sauce
for vegetables. Store
in refrigerator and
discard after 5 to 7
days.

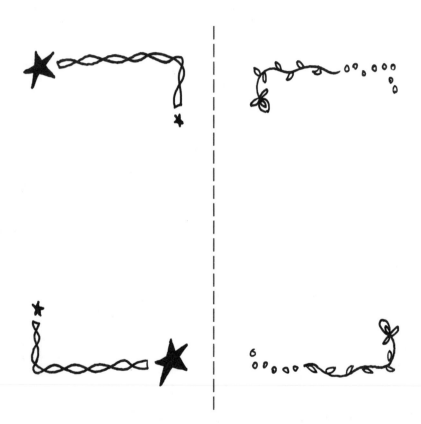

Blue Cheese Dressing

Makes 2 cups

1/2 C. cream cheese, softened
4 oz. blue cheese
6 T. mayonnaise
1/2 C. milk
1 T. chopped fresh parsley
1 T. chopped fresh chives
Pepper to taste

In a small bowl, combine softened cream cheese and blue cheese. Mix well. Transfer mixture to a blender or food processor. Add mayonnaise and milk. Blend well. Add fresh chopped parsley, fresh chopped chives and pepper. If necessary, add more milk until sauce reaches desired consistency. Using a funnel, transfer to a decorative sealable bottle and refrigerate. Will keep for 5 to 7 days in the refrigerator.

Attach a gift tag with directions on how to serve dressing.

Gift Tag Directions:

Blue Cheese Dressing

Toss Blue Cheese Dressing with salad greens or use as a dipping sauce for chicken wings or veggies. Store in refrigerator and discard after 5 to 7 days.

Blue Cheese Dressing

Toss Blue Cheese Dressing with salad greens or use as a dipping sauce for chicken wings or veggies. Store in refrigerator and discard after 5 to 7 days.

Blue Cheese Dressing

Toss Blue Cheese Dressing with salad greens or use as a dipping sauce for chicken wings or veggies. Store in refrigerator and discard after 5 to 7 days.

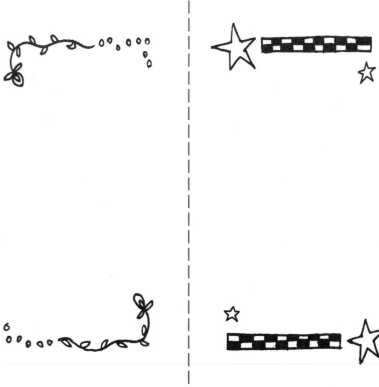

Blue Cheese Dressing

Toss Blue Cheese Dressing with salad greens or use as a dipping sauce for chicken wings or veggies. Store in refrigerator and discard after 5 to 7 days.

Blue Cheese Dressing

Toss Blue Cheese Dressing with salad greens or use as a dipping sauce for chicken wings or veggies. Store in refrigerator and discard after 5 to 7 days.

Sweet Bacon Dressing

Makes 3 cups

8 slices bacon
1 C. sugar
6 tsp. cornstarch
1 tsp. salt
1 C. water
1 1/2 C. distilled white vinegar

In a large skillet over medium high heat, cook bacon until evenly browned. Drain bacon and crumble into small pieces. In a medium bowl, combine sugar, cornstarch and salt with a whisk. Slowly add water and vinegar, whisking constantly. In a skillet, combine crumbled bacon and vinegar mixture. Cook over medium heat, stirring constantly, until mixture thickens slightly. Mixture will continue to thicken after removed from heat. Using a funnel, transfer to a decorative sealable bottle and refrigerate. Will keep for 3 to 5 days in the refrigerator.

Attach a gift tag with directions on how to serve dressing.

Gift Tag Directions:

Sweet Bacon Dressing

Toss Sweet Bacon Dressing
with salad greens or drizzle over
fresh cut cucumbers or carrots.
Store in refrigerator and discard
after 3 to 5 days.

Sweet Bacon Dressing

Toss Sweet Bacon Dressing with salad greens or drizzle over fresh cut cucumbers or carrots. Store in refrigerator and discard after 3 to 5 days.

Sweet Bacon Dressing

Toss Sweet Bacon Dressing with salad greens or drizzle over fresh cut cucumbers or carrots. Store in refrigerator and discard after 3 to 5 days.

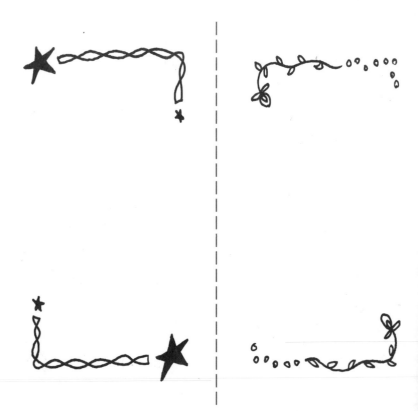

Sweet Bacon Dressing

Toss Sweet Bacon Dressing with salad greens or drizzle over fresh cut cucumbers or carrots. Store in refrigerator and discard after 3 to 5 days.

Sweet Bacon Dressing

Toss Sweet Bacon Dressing with salad greens or drizzle over fresh cut cucumbers or carrots. Store in refrigerator and discard after 3 to 5 days.

Honey-Poppy Seed Dressing

Makes 1 1/2 cups

1 (8 oz.) container plain yogurt
1 T. poppy seeds
1 T. honey
1 tsp. orange juice
1 1/2 tsp. apple cider vinegar
1/4 tsp. grated orange peel

In a large bowl, combine plain yogurt, poppy seeds, honey, orange juice, vinegar and grated orange peel. Mix until well blended. Using a funnel, transfer to a decorative sealable bottle and refrigerate. Will keep for 7 to 10 days in the refrigerator.

Attach a gift tag with directions on how to serve dressing.

Gift Tag Directions:

Honey-Poppy Seed Dressing

Toss Honey-Poppy Seed Dressing with salad greens or drizzle over fresh vegetables. Store in refrigerator and discard after 7 to 10 days.

Honey-Poppy Seed Dressing

Toss Honey-Poppy Seed Dressing with salad greens or drizzle over fresh vegetables. Store in refrigerator and discard after 7 to 10 days.

Honey-Poppy Seed Dressing

Toss Honey-Poppy Seed Dressing with salad greens or drizzle over fresh vegetables. Store in refrigerator and discard after 7 to 10 days.

Honey-Poppy Seed Dressing

Toss Honey-Poppy Seed Dressing with salad greens or drizzle over fresh vegetables. Store in refrigerator and discard after 7 to 10 days.

Honey-Poppy Seed Dressing

Toss Honey-Poppy Seed Dressing with salad greens or drizzle over fresh vegetables. Store in refrigerator and discard after 7 to 10 days.

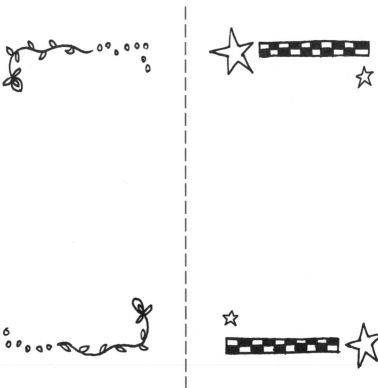

Asian Ginger Dressing

Makes 1 1/2 cups

3 cloves garlic, minced
2 T. minced ginger root
3/4 C. olive oil
1/3 C. rice vinegar
1/2 C. soy sauce
3 T. honey
2 T. water

In a blender or food processor, combine minced garlic, minced ginger root, olive oil, rice vinegar, soy sauce, honey and water. Process until dressing is smooth. Using a funnel, transfer to a decorative sealable bottle and refrigerate. Will keep in refrigerator for 3 to 5 days.

Attach a gift tag with directions on how to serve dressing.

Gift Tag Directions:

Asian Ginger Dressing

Shake Asian Ginger Dressing well before using. Toss with salad greens or use as a marinade for fresh seafood or chicken. Store in refrigerator and discard after 3 to 5 days.

Asian Ginger Dressing

Shake Asian Ginger Dressing well before using. Toss with salad greens or use as a marinade for fresh seafood or chicken. Store in refrigerator and discard after 3 to 5 days.

Asian Ginger Dressing

Shake Asian Ginger Dressing well before using. Toss with salad greens or use as a marinade for fresh seafood or chicken. Store in refrigerator and discard after 3 to 5 days.

Asian Ginger Dressing

Shake Asian Ginger Dressing well before using. Toss with salad greens or use as a marinade for fresh seafood or chicken. Store in refrigerator and discard after 3 to 5 days.

Asian Ginger Dressing

Shake Asian Ginger Dressing well before using. Toss with salad greens or use as a marinade for fresh seafood or chicken. Store in refrigerator and discard after 3 to 5 days.

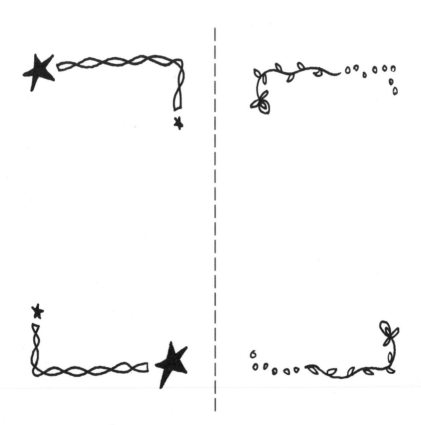

Augustus Caesar Dressing

Makes 3 cups

1 1/2 C. olive oil
1 T. red wine vinegar
1/4 C. lemon juice
1 T. Worcestershire sauce
1/2 tsp. mustard powder
1 tsp. ground garlic
3 T. sour cream
1/2 C. grated Parmesan cheese
2 T. anchovy paste, optional

In a blender or food processor, combine olive oil, vinegar, lemon juice, Worcestershire sauce, mustard powder, ground garlic, sour cream and grated Parmesan cheese. If desired, add anchovy paste. Process until dressing is smooth. Using a funnel, transfer to a decorative sealable bottle and refrigerate. Will keep in refrigerator for 3 to 5 days.

Attach a gift tag with directions on how to serve dressing.

Gift Tag Directions:

Augustus Caesar Dressing

To make a Caesar salad, toss Augustus Caesar Dressing with Romaine lettuce, croutons and shredded Romano cheese. Store dressing in refrigerator and discard after 3 to 5 days.

Augustus Caesar Dressing

To make a Caesar salad, toss Augustus Caesar Dressing with Romaine lettuce, croutons and shredded Romano cheese. Store dressing in refrigerator and discard after 3 to 5 days.

Augustus Caesar Dressing

To make a Caesar salad, toss Augustus Caesar Dressing with Romaine lettuce, croutons and shredded Romano cheese. Store dressing in refrigerator and discard after 3 to 5 days.

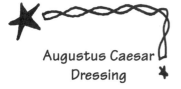

Augustus Caesar Dressing

To make a Caesar salad, toss Augustus Caesar Dressing with Romaine lettuce, croutons and shredded Romano cheese. Store dressing in refrigerator and discard after 3 to 5 days.

Augustus Caesar Dressing

To make a Caesar salad, toss Augustus Caesar Dressing with Romaine lettuce, croutons and shredded Romano cheese. Store dressing in refrigerator and discard after 3 to 5 days.

Russian Dressing

Makes 1 1/2 cups

1 C. mayonnaise
3 tsp. minced onions
1 tsp. prepared horseradish
1 tsp. Worcestershire sauce
1 tsp. dried parsley flakes
3 T. chili sauce
1 T. ketchup

In a blender or food processor, combine mayonnaise, minced onions, horseradish, Worcestershire sauce, dried parsley flakes, chili sauce and ketchup. Process until dressing is smooth. Using a funnel, transfer to a decorative sealable bottle and refrigerate. Will keep in refrigerator for 5 to 7 days.

Attach a gift tag with directions on how to serve dressing.

Gift Tag Directions:

Russian Dressing

Toss Russian Dressing with salad greens or use as a dipping sauce for vegetables. Store in refrigerator and discard after 5 to 7 days.

Russian Dressing

Toss Russian Dressing with salad greens or use as a dipping sauce for vegetables. Store in refrigerator and discard after 5 to 7 days.

Russian Dressing

Toss Russian Dressing with salad greens or use as a dipping sauce for vegetables. Store in refrigerator and discard after 5 to 7 days.

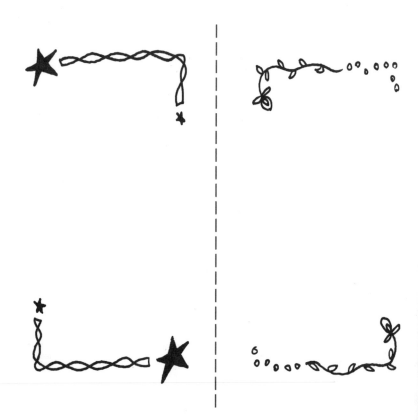

Russian Dressing

Toss Russian Dressing with salad greens or use as a dipping sauce for vegetables. Store in refrigerator and discard after 5 to 7 days.

Russian Dressing

Toss Russian Dressing with salad greens or use as a dipping sauce for vegetables. Store in refrigerator and discard after 5 to 7 days.

Pepper-Parmesan Dressing

Makes 2 cups

1/2 C. sour cream
3/4 C. low fat buttermilk
1/2 C. grated Parmesan cheese
2 cloves garlic, minced
6 T. white wine vinegar
1 1/2 T. pepper
2 pinches salt

In a blender or food processor, combine sour cream, buttermilk, grated Parmesan cheese, minced garlic, vinegar, pepper and salt. Process until dressing is smooth. Using a funnel, transfer to a decorative sealable bottle and refrigerate. Refrigerate at least 1 hour before serving. Will keep in refrigerator for 5 to 7 days.

Attach a gift tag with directions on how to serve dressing.

Gift Tag Directions:

Pepper-Parmesan Dressing

Toss Pepper-Parmesan Dressing with salad greens or use as a dipping sauce for vegetables. Store in refrigerator and discard after 5 to 7 days.

Pepper-Parmesan Dressing

Toss Pepper-Parmesan Dressing with salad greens or use as a dipping sauce for vegetables. Store in refrigerator and discard after 5 to 7 days.

Pepper-Parmesan Dressing

Toss Pepper-Parmesan Dressing with salad greens or use as a dipping sauce for vegetables. Store in refrigerator and discard after 5 to 7 days.

Pepper-Parmesan
Dressing

Toss Pepper-Parmesan Dressing with salad greens or use as a dipping sauce for vegetables. Store in refrigerator and discard after 5 to 7 days.

Pepper-Parmesan
Dressing

Toss Pepper-Parmesan Dressing with salad greens or use as a dipping sauce for vegetables. Store in refrigerator and discard after 5 to 7 days.

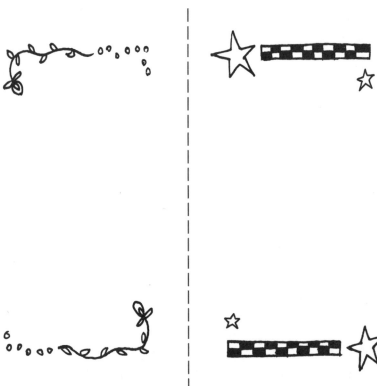

Seasoned Crunchy Cracker Topping

Makes 5 cups

1 (12 oz.) pkg. oyster crackers
1 1/2 T. dry ranch dressing mix
1 tsp. lemon pepper
1 tsp. dried dill
1/2 tsp. garlic salt

Crush oyster crackers by placing crackers between 2 paper towels and pressing down with a rolling pin. In a large bowl, combine crushed oyster crackers, ranch dressing mix, lemon pepper, dried dill and garlic salt. Toss well, until crackers are evenly coated. Using a funnel, transfer crackers to a decorative sealable bottle.

Attach a gift tag with directions on how to serve topping.

Suggested dressings to give with this salad topper are: Rosemary Thyme Vinegar (page 3), Fresh Dill Vinegar (page 5), Creamy Italian Dressing (page 15), Thousand Island Dressing (page 19) or Blue Cheese Dressing (page 21).

Gift Tag Directions:

Seasoned Crunchy
Cracker Topping

Sprinkle Seasoned Crunchy
Cracker Topping over salads or soups
for a tasty topping.

**Seasoned Crunchy
Cracker Topping**

Sprinkle Seasoned
Crunchy Cracker
Topping over salads or
soups for a tasty
topping.

**Seasoned Crunchy
Cracker Topping**

Sprinkle Seasoned
Crunchy Cracker
Topping over salads or
soups for a tasty
topping.

Seasoned Crunchy Cracker Topping

Sprinkle Seasoned Crunchy Cracker Topping over salads or soups for a tasty topping.

Seasoned Crunchy Cracker Topping

Sprinkle Seasoned Crunchy Cracker Topping over salads or soups for a tasty topping.

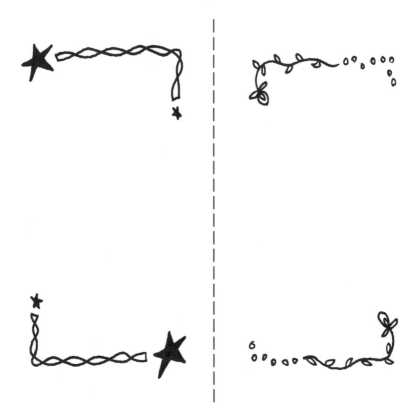

Walnut Cranberry Crunchies

Makes 3 1/2 cups

2 C. walnuts, finely chopped
3/4 C. sugar
1/4 C. water
1 1/2 C. dried cranberries or craisins, chopped

Lightly grease a baking sheet and set aside. In a medium bowl, combine finely chopped walnuts, sugar and water. Cook in microwave for 8 to 8 1/2 minutes, stirring after every 1 to 2 minutes, until sugar has caramelized. Pour walnuts onto prepared baking sheet and separate into little pieces. Let walnuts cool completely. In a large bowl, combine sugar glazed walnuts and dried cranberries. Mix until well blended. Using a funnel, transfer to a decorative sealable bottle, breaking pieces if necessary.

Attach a gift tag with directions on how to serve topping.

Suggested dressings to give with this salad topper are: Blackberry Vinegar (page 1), Raspberry Vinegar (page 9), Cranberry Vinegar (page 11), Sweet Bacon Dressing (page 23) or Honey-Poppy Seed Dressing (page 25).

Gift Tag Directions:

Walnut Cranberry Crunchies

Sprinkle Walnut Cranberry
Crunchies over salads for a tasty
and sweet topping.

Walnut Cranberry Crunchies

Sprinkle Walnut Cranberry Crunchies over salads for a tasty and sweet topping.

Walnut Cranberry Crunchies

Sprinkle Walnut Cranberry Crunchies over salads for a tasty and sweet topping.

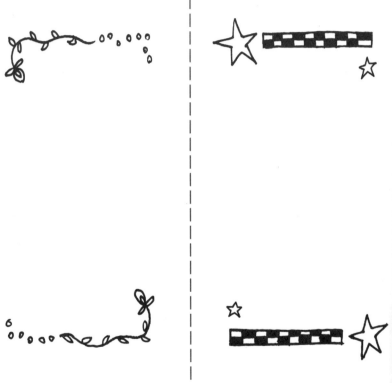

Walnut Cranberry Crunchies

Sprinkle Walnut Cranberry Crunchies over salads for a tasty and sweet topping.

Walnut Cranberry Crunchies

Sprinkle Walnut Cranberry Crunchies over salads for a tasty and sweet topping.

The Ultimate Salad Topper

Makes 3 cups

1 C. bacon bits
1 (.05 oz.) container dried chopped chives
1 C. sunflower seeds
1 C. broken chow mein noodles

In a large bowl, combine bacon bits, dried chopped chives, sunflower seeds and broken chow mein noodles. Using a funnel, transfer to a decorative sealable bottle.

Attach a gift tag with directions on how to serve topping.

Suggested dressings to give with this salad topper are: Herbal Vinegar (page 7), Ranch Dressing (page 17), Blue Cheese Dressing (page 21), Asian Ginger Dressing (page 27) or Russian Dressing (page 31).

Gift Tag Directions:

The Ultimate Salad Topper

Sprinkle The Ultimate Salad Topper over salads for a tasty and crunchy topping.

The Ultimate
Salad Topper

Sprinkle The
Ultimate Salad
Topper over salads
for a tasty and
crunchy topping.

The Ultimate
Salad Topper

Sprinkle The
Ultimate Salad
Topper over salads
for a tasty and
crunchy topping.

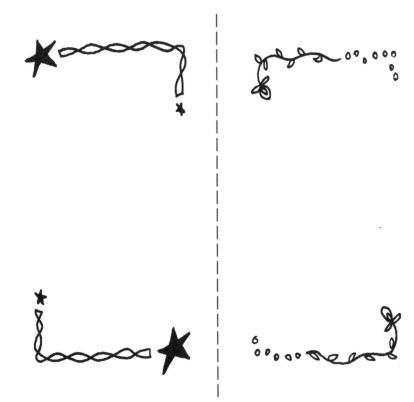

**The Ultimate
Salad Topper**

Sprinkle The
Ultimate Salad
Topper over salads
for a tasty and
crunchy topping.

**The Ultimate
Salad Topper**

Sprinkle The
Ultimate Salad
Topper over salads
for a tasty and
crunchy topping.

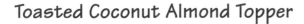

Toasted Coconut Almond Topper

Makes 3 cups

1 C. slivered almonds, chopped
2 T. sugar, divided
2 C. flaked coconut

Preheat oven to 350°. Lightly grease 2 baking sheets. On 1 baking sheet, place chopped slivered almonds evenly in a single layer. Sprinkle 1 tablespoon sugar over almonds. Bake for approximately 10 minutes, until almonds are golden brown. Place flaked coconut evenly in a single layer on the other baking sheet. Sprinkle remaining 1 tablespoon sugar over coconut. Bake for approximately 5 to 7 minutes, stirring occasionally, until coconut is golden brown. In a bowl, combine almonds and coconut. Using a funnel, transfer to a decorative sealable bottle.

Attach a gift tag with directions on how to serve topping.

Suggested dressings to give with this salad topper are: Blackberry Vinegar (page 1), Raspberry Vinegar (page 9), Sweet Bacon Dressing (page 23) or Asian Ginger Dressing (page 27).

Gift Tag Directions:

Toasted Coconut Almond Topper

Sprinkle Toasted Coconut Almond
Topper over salads for a tasty topping.

**Toasted Coconut
Almond Topper**

Sprinkle Toasted
Coconut Almond
Topper over salads
for a tasty topping.

**Toasted Coconut
Almond Topper**

Sprinkle Toasted
Coconut Almond
Topper over salads
for a tasty topping.

Toasted Coconut
Almond Topper

Sprinkle Toasted
Coconut Almond
Topper over salads
for a tasty topping.

Toasted Coconut
Almond Topper

Sprinkle Toasted
Coconut Almond
Topper over salads
for a tasty topping.

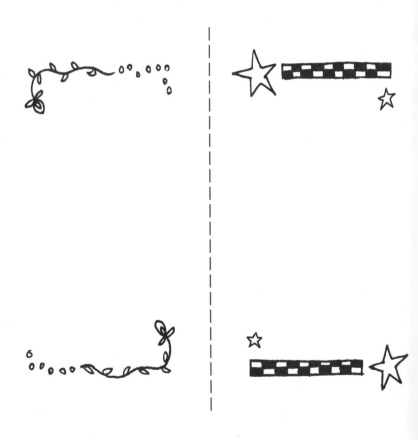

Index

Recipes Shown on Front Cover

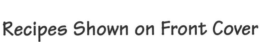

From left to right